Boy

GREYSTONE BOOKS

Douglas & McIntyre Publishing Group

Vancouver/Toronto/Berkeley

Ainslie Manson

Illustrated by
Renné Benoit

in **Motion**

RICK HANSEN'S STORY

ONCE there was a boy who hated to sit down.
"You must at least sit down to eat," his
mother would say.

"I don't have time to sit," he would reply, as he
bounced a ball across the hall and out the door
into the sunshine.

This boy, whose name was Rick, was always
in motion.

One day, Rick's parents told him they were taking him camping.

The first morning, he was up before the sun. He burst from the tent and rushed to the beach. A massive gleaming salmon arched high out of the water.

"Dad!" Rick bellowed. "I've just seen the biggest fish in the whole wide world, and I'm going to catch it."

"We didn't bring a fishing rod," said his father.

"We can make one, Dad! Quick, quick!"

The whole family got involved. Rick and his brother, Brad, found just the right willow tree.

"Perfect," said his father, cutting a branch for the rod.

"And here's your fishing line," said his mother, handing over a piece of string.

Rick's baby sister gurgled as they removed a pin from her diaper to use as a fishing hook.

Rick did not catch a fish that day. Or the next. He didn't even get a bite. But he *was* bitten. He was bitten by the fishing bug.

When Rick had grown a little bigger and a little stronger, his father took him on a long hike to an extra-special fishing lake. Loons cried on the crystal-clear water, and minnows darted in the shallows.

His dad pointed to a small raft moored at the end of a fallen cedar tree. Rick's heart pounded. The round, slippery tree trunk seemed to stretch on forever.

"I can't!" said Rick.

"There's no such word as can't," said his father. "Don't look down; just keep going, one step at a time."

A fish jumped far out in the lake. Rick clenched his teeth and set off.

At the end of the day, he crept back along the fallen tree in semi-darkness, being extra careful not to drop his catch—a string of five shining rainbow trout.

When he wasn't fishing, Rick was pitching or tossing or kicking or batting a ball of some sort. He played basketball, volleyball, and football. He was proud of his skills. Rick loved all sports, but when he was fifteen, volleyball was his favorite.

"I want you to try out for the championship team next weekend," said his coach.

Rick frowned. He had made plans with his friends Randy and Don to go on a week-long fishing trip. It was a hard choice, but there would be another tryout soon. So Rick chose to go fishing. That bite from the fishing bug still itched.

It was a perfect week, but when it was over, the three
boys were tired, dirty, and hungry. They were eager to
get home. They drove partway with Randy in his truck.
But from Randy's house, Rick and Don still had a long
way to go.

"Should we hitchhike?"

"No, we'd better not."

"But just think, we'd be there in time for dinner."

"And we should get these fish home . . ."

They accepted a ride in the back of a rusty old truck.

Despite the dust and discomfort, Rick fell asleep.
But not for long. On a dangerous curve, the truck hit a
bumpy patch, flew off the road, and flipped over.

At the side of the road, Rick slammed into the
sharp edge of the truck's metal toolbox. Everything else
came down on top of him . . . the contents of the truck,
pain, panic, and darkness.

When he came to, he couldn't feel his legs. He
had never been so afraid.

The ambulance. The hospital. It was all a bad dream.

"I doubt you'll ever walk again," the doctor said.

Rick's head swam, but he laughed. He was an athlete. Break a bone, get it fixed. Right?

For eight weeks, he lay on a bed called a Stryker frame. Every three hours the nurses turned him, like a chicken on a spit.

When his friends came to visit, he laughed at their glum faces. "Hey guys, I'll be home soon!" he'd say.

Only his parents saw the nighttime Rick.

"Make them do something," he pleaded.

His parents stood at the foot of Rick's bed. Their boy who hated to sit down was now begging to sit up, and there was nothing they could do.

Rick was paralyzed below the waist. He was a paraplegic.

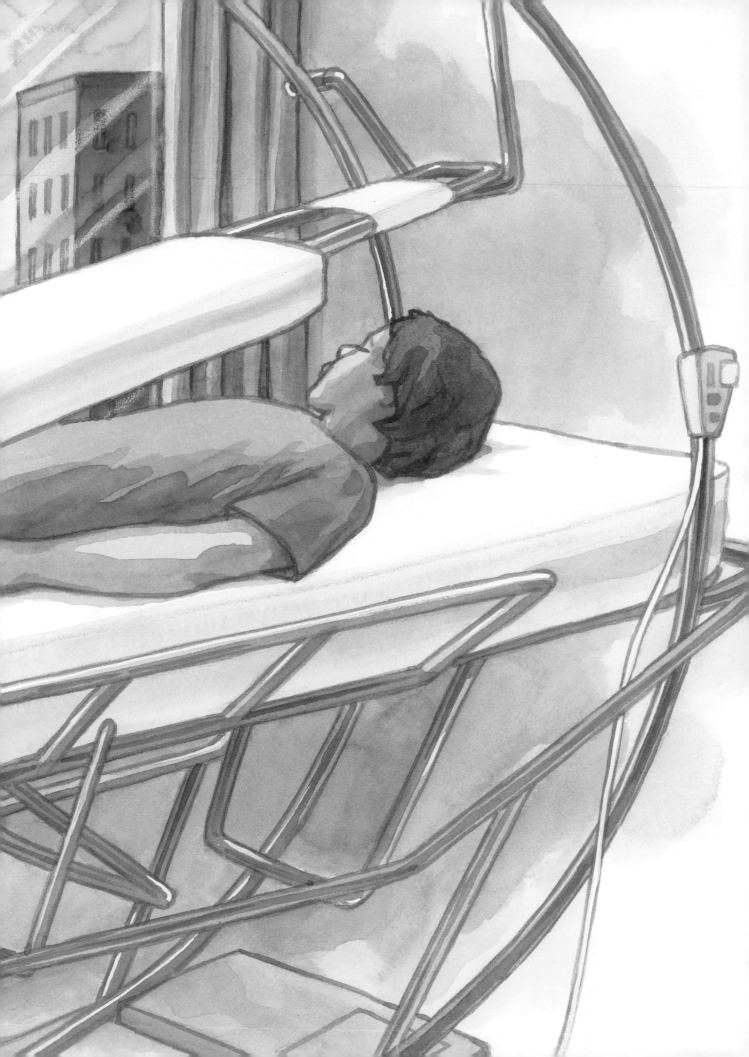

At first, the weeks crawled by. Then at long last, Rick was given a wheelchair. He was in motion again!

Next, he was fitted with leg braces. "Look, I'm walking!" he announced.

"It's really more like balancing and hopping," a physiotherapist explained. "With braces and crutches you'll not be breaking speed limits like you do in your wheelchair."

He would prove them wrong! He practiced for hours each day.

"Go to bed!" the staff would insist when he was still clattering up and down flights of stairs at ten o'clock.

Rick's walking did improve, but in the end he realized the physios were right. The crutches made him more independent, but they slowed him down.

In a wheelchair, he became a pro. He learned to do wheelies. He built up speed. He even began to fool around with a basketball.

After seven long months, it was time to go home.

"You drive," said his dad, tossing him the keys to a brand new Ford Bronco with special hand controls.

Rick squared his chin and transferred into the driver's seat. Driving with hand controls was easy. He'd taken lessons. But as they drove north, the weather grew harsh, and the hand controls kept sticking. Rick was haunted by memories of flying off the road.

"Dad, you'd better take over," he said. "I can't do it."

"There's no such word as can't," his father said, crossing his arms and staring straight ahead. Rick gripped the wheel and drove on. Even when they skidded into a snowbank, he didn't give up.

It was good to be home, good to taste his mother's cooking again. But the doors and hallways were too narrow, and there were no wheelchair ramps or elevators.

"Come on, Rick, you can do it!" Brad would shout as he watched his brother working his way almost to the top of the stairs. Several times, the banister pulled right out of the wall, and down Rick went, head over heels, all the way to the bottom.

Everyone laughed . . . even Rick. But it wasn't really funny.

Home was hard, but school was worse. He remembered how he'd tried not to stare at a boy struggling to walk after recovering from polio. He'd felt pity. But Rick didn't want pity—not one bit.

One winter day, as he took a shortcut between two school buildings, his feet flew out from under him. "They'll find me in the spring," he said aloud as snowflakes fell on his face.

Then two classmates came along. They grinned at him and heaved him to his feet. Could it be that they were seeing the same old Rick, crutches and all?

Rick was surrounded by family and friends, but he still felt like the loneliest person on earth.

His family longed to ease his sadness.

"Let's go fishing," his dad suggested one day.

"It'll be cool," said Brad.

Rick wondered.

"They could have chosen an easier spot," he muttered to himself as his dad led the way across a rickety swinging bridge.

He groaned as he crutched his way along two miles of railway track.

And he complained bitterly when they anchored him to a tree so that he could fish from the steep bank without falling headfirst into the water.

Then he forgot the muttering, the groaning, and the complaining. He was fishing again, and it was awesome!

Rick's teachers and coaches encouraged him to stay involved in sports. Rick wasn't sure.

"Come and help us with the coaching," one of them suggested.

They kept at him until he gave in. He found he liked teaching. It felt good to be back in his old school gym. It felt great to be helping the players.

"What are your plans for after graduation?" a teacher asked him.

Rick shrugged. "Well, I won't be going to university now."

"Oh? And why is that?"

"I had planned to be a phys ed teacher," said Rick, staring at the ground.

"Fantastic!" said the teacher. "Go for it!"

When Rick was in grade eleven, a pioneer in the
field of wheelchair sports came to visit.

"I hear you're a good athlete," he said. "I think you
should come down to the city for a little competition."

Competition. Rick couldn't resist.

"Let's get the ball rolling," the man said.

Rick didn't ask which ball. He'd be happy with any.

A month later, he had his first gold medal around his neck. He'd won it playing table tennis.

Next, he tried wheelchair basketball. He began wheeling long distances to make himself a stronger player. Soon a new interest developed: a passion for track and marathons.

"There may be a thousand things I'll never be able to do again," he could now say, "but there are ten thousand things I can still do."

At university, Rick grew more and more independent. He was always in motion, constantly playing sports or training, and he was traveling a lot. His volleyball team took first place in the Canadian Wheelchair Games. Then he went to England and played basketball in the World Games.

One weekend, when he was back at home, he decided
to go fishing on his own. He'd manage, no problem.

"One last hill and I'm there," he said, once he had
mastered a five-foot fence and a locked gate.

But that final steep hill defeated the challenge master.
He picked up too much speed. Faster and faster he flew,
right over the bank and into the river.

He was up to his neck in water and over his head in trouble. He had to act fast. He grabbed his chair just before it sank and used all his strength to fling it onto the bank. Then, slipping and sliding and grabbing at tufts of grass, he hauled himself up after it.

For a long moment, he lay on the grass gasping.

Then he went fishing. Why not?

He wasn't going to miss a chance to catch fish just because he was wet and weary.

Rick did catch fish that afternoon, but as often happened when he was by a river, he also caught hold of his dreams. He saw himself wheeling a long, long distance. A smile spread across his face.

"Hear this!" he shouted to the fish and the birds and a cow in a nearby field. "I just might wheel all the way around the world!"

He laughed as he packed up his fishing rod. Now that would be my kind of challenge, he thought.

Afterword

As Rick traveled in North America and in Europe, he experienced again and again how hard it was to get around in a wheelchair. He began to wonder if there was some way he could help to bring about change.

Rick was inspired by Terry Fox. Terry died after raising much awareness and money for cancer research on his cross-Canada marathon. Rick and Terry had been good friends and had played wheelchair basketball together. Rick was deeply saddened by his friend's death, but he realized that Terry had achieved his goal even though his run was cut short when his cancer returned. His dream would go on forever as people ran in the annual Terry Fox Run.

He thought about his own dream. He wanted to make the public aware of people with disabilities. Perhaps at the same time he could raise money to help people with spinal cord injury.

Rick's dream became a reality. The Man In Motion World Tour set off from Vancouver, British Columbia, on March 21, 1985. The team was made up of many people, each with a different role.

Each day Rick wheeled the equivalent of two marathons, often with one of the others cycling beside him. They were on the road in all kinds of weather. Rick's arms ached; his hands blistered. It never got easier, but he did grow stronger.

They traveled through thirty-four countries. The tour took two years, two months, and two days. They raised over $26 million, and Rick's message was spread far and wide.

Crowds welcomed them home: hundreds of thousands of people in Vancouver alone.

And when the tour was over, Rick didn't stop. His goals and his dreams grew and grew. The boy in motion had become a man, a man in never-ending motion.

Facts and Figures

about Rick Hansen and the Man In Motion World Tour

› Rick was born in Port Alberni, British Columbia, and grew up in Williams Lake.

› He won nineteen international wheelchair marathons, including three world championships.

› He and Wayne Gretzky shared Canada's outstanding athlete of the year award (the Lou Marsh Award) in 1983.

› In 1984, he represented Canada in the Olympic Games in Los Angeles, competing in the finals of the 1,500-meter wheelchair race.

› Rick was the first student with a physical disability to graduate in Phys Ed from the University of British Columbia.

› Rick wheeled 40,075 kilometers during the Man In Motion World Tour—a distance equal to the circumference of the earth.

› The goal of the Man In Motion World Tour was to encourage people to make communities more accessible and inclusive for those with disabilities and to find a cure for spinal cord injury. Rick changed people's perceptions about the potential of those with disabilities and about what is possible for anyone who dreams big dreams and has the determination to see them through.

› Amanda Reid was an important member of the Man In Motion team, both as Rick's physiotherapist and as an integral member of tour management on the road. Halfway around the world, Rick and Amanda became engaged, and they were married when they returned home. Rick, Amanda, and their three daughters live in Richmond, British Columbia.

› Rick became a Companion of the Order of Canada in 1988.

› He is president and CEO of the Rick Hansen Foundation. The Foundation is committed to improving the quality of life of people living with spinal cord injury.

› Rick volunteers his time as chair of the Fraser River Sturgeon Conservation Society and the Pacific Salmon Endowment Fund Society.

To learn more about Rick, the Man In Motion World Tour, and Rick's ongoing work through the Rick Hansen Foundation, visit www.rickhansen.com.

*In memory of my friend and fellow writer Sandra Richmond,
another challenge master. —A.M.*

*For my mother, for taking me to see Rick Hansen wheel through
Bells Corners on his inspirational Man In Motion World Tour
when I was nine. —R.B.*

Greystone Books
A division of Douglas & McIntyre Ltd.
2323 Quebec Street, Suite 201
Vancouver, British Columbia
Canada v5t 4s7
www.greystonebooks.com

Library and Archives Canada Cataloguing in Publication
Manson, Ainslie
Boy in motion : Rick Hansen's story / Ainslie Manson ;
illustrated by Renné Benoit.

ISBN 978-1-55365-252-6

1. Hansen, Rick, 1957– —Juvenile literature. 2. Paraplegics—Canada—Biography—Juvenile
literature. 3. Athletes with disabilities—Canada—Biography. I. Benoit, Renné II. Title.
RD796.H35M35 2006   j362.4'3092   C2006-905494-0

Editing by Maggie de Vries
Jacket design by Peter Cocking
Text design by Peter Cocking/Naomi MacDougall/Katy Sigalet
Jacket illustration by Renné Benoit
Printed and bound in China by C&C Offset Printing Co., Ltd.
Printed on acid-free paper
Distributed in the U.S. by Publishers Group West

We gratefully acknowledge the financial support of the Canada Council for the Arts, the
British Columbia Arts Council, the Province of British Columbia through the Book
Publishing Tax Credit, and the Government of Canada through the Book Publishing Industry
Development Program (BPIDP) for our publishing activities.